Contents

Build A Vocabulary That Works For You

Introduction

Why should you want to learn more words? You're not trying to impress anybody, so what good will it do you? Those are fair questions. And here are some answers — good reasons for learning more words.

Higher Test Scores

Standardized tests have become a fact of life — not just in school, but in the workplace as well. From the time you start elementary school (and often even earlier), all the way through your application for a job or graduate school, you're judged in part by how well you score on standardized tests.

In the workplace, we find that many employers are using standardized tests for hiring, and as one criterion for promotions and selection to certain jobs.

Studies have repeatedly shown that vocabulary skills are clearly tied to better scores on standardized tests, from the PSAT to the GRE.

Better Grades

A good general vocabulary will help you express yourself in writing, oral reports, and class discussions. And improving your knowledge of words used in the subjects you're studying has obvious value. No matter what subject you're studying, learning the words commonly used in that subject will help you understand the subject, and will certainly help you make better grades.

A Higher IQ score

Does that claim sound like false advertising? It isn't. There's a lot of argument about so-called intelligence tests (or IQ tests, for *intelligence quotient*). But almost everyone who's familiar with the tests will agree with this statement: *people who have better vocabularies make higher scores on IQ tests.* Most IQ tests are made up of several subtests covering topics such as mathematical calculations, spatial relations, and vocabulary. Of all subtests, the one that is most highly correlated to the total IQ score is the one that measures vocabulary.

5

More Career Success, Higher Income

This is not just guessing. One of my favorite vocabulary books reported on a study, by the Human Engineering Laboratory, which said that the *only* common characteristic of highly successful people is an unusual knowledge of words. On the average, people with better vocabularies have more successful careers, get more promotions, and earn more money.

You'll Be Smarter

You won't just *appear* smarter, you'll actually *be* smarter. And this is not the same as simply increasing your IQ score. When you learn a new word, you don't just learn an isolated definition. In most cases, you are actually learning new information. Example: When you first learned the word *photosynthesis*, you didn't just learn a definition, you learned that plants use water and carbon dioxide to make sugars and other nutrients. That made you a little bit smarter. And with each new word you learn, you're increasing your knowledge.

It's Fun

Even though this one is last on the list, it's one of the best reasons for learning new words. Simply having fun is one of the most important things in life. People who make time to do things that bring them pleasure are happier, healthier, and more satisfied with their lives.

Learning words, playing with them, tossing them back and forth among your friends — this is a lot of fun. And it can keep on being fun, and paying off for you, for the rest of your life.

Unit 1 – People and Their Personalities

There's an old saying: "It takes all kinds of people to make a world." And we could add: "Yes, and they're all here."

People are fascinating. How they think and act, what they're interested in, how they look, and how they treat us. We want to know these things about our fellow humans. The answers often surprise us, and always interest us.

And among the most interesting things about people are their personalities — how they act and react around other people. Are they outgoing, party-people who love to be around others? Or are they loners, people who prefer to find a quiet place where they can be alone?

How do they treat us? Are they aggressive and competitive, always trying to get ahead of us? Or do they try to be helpful? Do they make us feel liked and trusted, or do they look at us with mistrust or even hatred?

Some of these people you'll like, some you won't. But sooner or later you're going to meet all these personality types — whether you want to or not. So let's look at a few words to describe them.

Misanthrope: *"People are no good."* You know him. And you wish you didn't. He hates everybody. He's always looking for the worst in everyone — and finding it. You mention something nice another person has done, and he'll scoff and tell you how the person was really doing it for selfish reasons. He doesn't seem to trust anybody, or to like anybody — maybe not even himself.

He's a **misanthrope.** The word's pronounced MISS-un-thrope, and it's made up of two Greek elements. The first is *misein* (meaning *to hate*, often shortened to *mis* in English words), and the second is *anthropos* (man, person).

Related word: He has a *misanthropic* (mis-un-THROP-ik) outlook on life.

7

Altruist: *"I love people."* You know her, too — if you're lucky. She loves everybody. She's just the opposite of the misanthrope — making us feel good about her, ourselves, and maybe even the rest of the world. We're always glad to get away from the misanthrope, and we're just as glad to meet up with the altruist. She's always finding the best in other people, always seeming to find something good in them, something to like.

The word is pronounced AL-true-ist. That *ist* is a common ending for words that tell us about a person — usually about what that person does, or thinks, or believes, or loves. And the altruist loves *others* — which is what the root *alter* means.

Related words: She does *altruistic* (al-true-ISS-tik) things, because she's filled with *altruism* (AL-true-ism).

Egotist: *"Let's talk about me."* The two parts of this word pretty much tell it all. The *ist* means that the word refers to a person, and the *ego* (which means *self*) tells us what the person is interested in.

So the major interest of the egotist (EE-go-tist) is himself. His favorite words are *I*, *me*, and *myself*. When you're with him, you probably won't get to talk much, because he thinks that what he has to say is much too important to be interrupted by listening to anyone else. So he'll take over the conversation as soon as he can. And what does he talk about? Himself, of course — what he's done lately, how clever he is, how athletic, how handsome, how all the women like him, and on and on.

Related words: He has a big *ego*, his *egotism* can be irritating, he's an *egotistical* person.

Gregarious: *"Let's party."* People usually like the gregarious (gruh-GARE-ee-us) person, because she likes people. And she likes to have people around her. Instead of staying home and settling in with a good book or video, she'd much prefer to get together with a bunch of friends.

The root of this word is *greg*, which means *herd*. Gregarious animals live in herds, while solitary animals spend most of their time alone.

Recluse: *"Two's a crowd."* This person is not at all gregarious — just the opposite. The recluse (RECK-loose) hates crowds — even small groups. He likes to be by himself, and tries to lead a solitary life, staying away from people as much as possible.

Related words: Another word that means much the same is *hermit*, a person who leads a *reclusive* life (pronounced re-KLOOS-iv).

Introvert: *"I look inward."* Some people are always focused on others, on what's going on in the world around them. The introvert (EN-tro-vert), on the other hand, spends a lot of time looking inside herself — examining her own thoughts, feelings, doubts, and wishes.

But she's not an egotist, she's not in love with herself. In fact she may be full of self-doubt, and is often quiet and shy. Introverts may be good friends, but they are often happier being with others one-on-one or in small groups.

Breaking the word into its parts can help us understand and remember it. *Intro* means *into, inward*. And *vert* means *turn*. So the introverted person is *turned inward*.

Related words: She's an *introverted* person, her *introversion* sometimes makes people think she's unfriendly (but she's probably not).

Extrovert: *"Tell me about yourself."* Extro, the first part of this word, means outward. So the extrovert (EKS-tro-vert) is the opposite of the introvert. His attention is turned out to the world and people around him. He's happy around others, and likes to be involved in doing things with other people.

He is not shy, but neither is he an egotist. He almost always likes other people, and is likely to be very popular himself, because he's usually cheery, talkative, and interested in everyone he meets.

Related words: His *extroversion* (eks-tro-VER-zhun) helped make him a popular student.

Ambivert: *"Let's talk about you and me."* Most of us are neither introverts nor extroverts. Instead, our thoughts are sometimes turned inward, sometimes outward. So the word (AM-buh-vert) fits, because *ambi* means both. And this person looks both ways.

Instead of focusing entirely on looking inward or outward, the ambivert looks in both directions. She's not likely to be either unusually shy or egotistical. Instead, she's interested in other people *and* in herself.

Misogynist: *"Women are just no good."* There's that *mis* again, meaning *hatred* or *against*. And the *ist* tells us that it's a person — a person who hates, in this case. Who or what does the misogynist hate? The *gyn* means *woman*, so the misogynist is a woman-hater.

To pronounce the word, say *massage* (like a back-rub), and add *un-ist*.

Related word: His *misogynistic* (massage-un-IST-ik) attitude cost him the women's vote.

Misogamist: *"Marriage — humbug."* Marriage may be a fine institution, but who wants to live in an institution? This word looks a lot like *misogynist*, but it's definitely different. The *miso* and *ist* tell us that the word refers to a person who hates something or someone. But the misogamist (muh-SOG-um-ist) doesn't hate women (and may even *be* a woman). Instead the object of hatred is marriage, which is what the root *gamos* literally means. (We find it in *polygamy*, which means plural marriage, and in *bigamy*, illegally marrying a person while already married to someone else.)

Ascetic: *"I like simplicity."* This work comes from a Greek term meaning *monk*, or *hermit*. And if you think of the kind of life a monk may lead — a bare and simple room, plain clothes, food in small portions, and definitely not fancy — you have a good idea of what the *ascetic* wants out of life. Just the bare essentials, with no desire for what many of us call the finer things of life. This is a person who is more likely to spend time in lonely contemplation (as in religious study) than in doing things that most of us would call fun. The word's pronounced uh-SET-ik, and may be a noun (a person, in this case) or an adjective (He leads an ascetic life).

Voluptuary: *"I love the rich life."* If the ascetic is at one end of the lifestyle yardstick, the voluptuary (vol-UP-chew-ery) is at the other. She's not into hard work, or putting up with anything that's just so-so. She doesn't shop at discount stores, or ride the bus, or eat at fast-food places, but wants the best in fancy food and fine wine, classical music, expensive art, luxury housing. In short, she wants the best of everything, and lives for the finer things of life.

Luddite: *"Who needs progress?"* According to an old story, a man named Ned Lud (or Ludd) smashed labor-saving devices that threatened to eliminate jobs. So anyone who hates technological advances may be called a *luddite* (LUDD-ite).

Exercise 1 – A: People and Their Personalities

> **Directions:** In each item below, you'll find two terms, separated by a virgule (/), that are related in some way (e.g., long/short). A third ("single") term is separated by a virgule from a series of terms in parentheses. For each item, circle the term in parentheses that has *the same relationship* to the "single" term as the paired terms have to each other.

1. altruist/misanthrope = extrovert/ *(egotist, geek, ambivert, introvert)*

2. egotism/ *(shyness, self-centeredness, reclusiveness, introspection)* = rich/wealthy

3. velocity/speed = voluptuary/ *(progress-lover, people-hater, luxury-lover, woman-hater)*

4. voluptuary/ascetic = *(woman-hater, woman-lover, people-hater, people-lover)*/misogynist

5. extrovert/ *(shy guy, party animal, luddite, voluptuary)* = most/least

6. *(student, teacher, hermit, artist)*/recluse = extrovert/party person

7. misogamist/marriage-hater = *(masseuse, woman-hater, physical therapist, progress-hater)*/misogynist

8. introvert/ambivert = few/ *(most, all, none, some)*

9. happy/joyful = recluse/ *(party animal, hermit, bachelor, student)*

10. sweet/sour = technology-lover/ *(luddite, misogynist, misogamist, recluse)*

Exercise 1 – B: People and Their Personalities

> **Directions:** Write a letter in each blank, to match the words in the first column with the quotes in the second column.

Who?	**Says What?**
_____ 1. voluptuary	a. "I like meeting and talking with people."
_____ 2. egotist	b. "People are just no good."
_____ 3. altruist	c. "No wedding bells for me."
_____ 4. introvert	d. "I love good food, wine, and comfort."
_____ 5. extrovert	e. "No party, no wine, nothing fancy."
_____ 6. ambivert	f. "Have I told you how talented I am?"
_____ 7. misanthrope	g. "I'm interested in my friends and myself."
_____ 8. misogynist	h. "I care about people, and like to help them."
_____ 9. misogamist	i. "Women are just no good."
_____ 10. ascetic	j. "I spend a lot of time on introspection."

Exercise I – C: Write the Word

1. I hate women. Most men are all right, but the female of our species is definitely *not* okay. I'm a/an _____.

2. I like members of the opposite sex okay. But don't talk to me about marriage — I hate the very idea. I'm a/an _____.

3. Some people hate women, some hate men, some hate marriage. Me, I hate *everybody*. I'm a/an _____.

4. What good's all that hate stuff? I really like people. I think they're basically good, and I like to help and encourage others whenever I can. I'm a/an _____.

5. I hate newfangled things, like new machines and computers. These so-called technological advances are a pain, and I'd like to blow them all up. I'm a/an_____.

6. I'm a somewhat shy guy (or woman). I don't like crowds, parties, or dealing with people. I can tolerate being around others, but I prefer to spend a lot of time looking inside myself. I'm a/an

   _____.

7. I love parties, meeting others, talking with folks. I'm a/an

   _____.

8. What I really like is the good life. Give me a gourmet meal, with fine wine, a soft place to sit or lie, some good music, and I'm completely happy. I'm a/an _____.

9. None of that rich living for me. I much prefer the simple life — simple food (and not too much of that), simple clothing, just the bare necessities. I'm a/an _____.

10. I don't like to be around other people at all. If I could, I'd be a hermit, and go live completely by myself. I'm a/an _____.

Unit 2 – It's About Time

The words in this section are about time, and our attitudes toward it.

Procrastinate: Never do today what you can put off till tomorrow. When there's a job that needs doing, some of us want to jump right in and get it done, so we can relax afterward. The term paper is finished early, the tax forms are mailed way before the deadline, and the bags are packed in plenty of time.

But on the other hand, some people (not us, of course) like to procrastinate (pro-KRAS-tuh-nate). They'll put off the assigned paper until right before it's due, and may stay up all night getting it ready. They're always waiting until the last minute, and then rushing to finish in time. Related words: *procrastination, procrastinator.*

Anachronism: Pronounced uh-NACK-ruh-niz'm, this word refers to something out of place in time. A computer in a movie about the 1920's would be anachronistic. So would a dinosaur in modern times.

Diurnal: This word means "once a day, every day." It's used for things that happen daily — the sunrise is diurnal (dye-URN-ul), and of course so is nightfall. The word is also used for things that happen during the daytime, as opposed to night time. Diurnal flowers are open during daylight, and closed at night.

Nocturnal: This word (nock-TUR-nul) applies to things that go bump in the night. Or things that go out at night, period. Most owls are nocturnal, and so are many other animals. Even some flowers are nocturnal, opening their blossoms at night. And you probably know some people who like to stay up late at night, and aren't at their best during the daytime. We could call these night-owl friends nocturnal people.

Related word: *nocturne* — a painting of a night scene, or a dreamy song suggesting the stillness of night.

Crepuscular: This means neither diurnal nor nocturnal, but in between. Some creatures, including certain insects and birds, are most active during the brief time between daylight and dark (twilight), and just before sunrise in the morning.

Such creatures are called *crepuscular* (kruh-PUS-cue-lur). This is a word that isn't often used, but when it's needed, no other word will quite work.

Sidereal: One common way to measure time is by the movements of planets, stars, and other heavenly bodies — including the earth. When we think of a day as the time between sunrise yesterday and sunrise this morning, we're dealing in sidereal (side-EAR-ee-ul) time. That's okay for most of our purposes, but it has its problems. For one thing, that sidereal day isn't exactly 24 hours long. (It's about 23 hours, 56 minutes, and 4.1 seconds.) A sidereal month is about 27.32 days long, and a sidereal year lasts about 365 days, 6 hours, 9 minutes, and 9.54 seconds. That's one reason we have leap year — to help bring things (like clocks and calendars) back into balance.

Synchronous: This word means "at the same time." This word combines two very useful word elements, *syn* (which means *same)*, and *chron* (which means *time)*.

Related words: *synchronize* (to synchronize watches means to set them at the same time), *synchronicity* (the occurrence of two events at the same time), *chronometer* (a watch, clock, or similar time-keeping device).

We also have the words *contemporary* (often used to refer to someone who was living at the same time, as in "Ben Jonson was a contemporary of Shakespeare"), and *concurrent* (happening at the same time, as in "There will be two concurrent concerts, in different rooms").

Precedent: It's been said that what's past is prologue. In our system of law, judges often base their decisions on court records of similar cases in the past. Such cases are called *precedents* (PRESS-uh-dunts). If something happens for the first time (as when the first baseball player hits 70 home runs in a season), it's called an *unprecedented* event.

Related words: Precede (to go or happen before), precedence (pronounced either PRESS-uh-dunts, or pre-CEED-unce), meaning having priority because of some higher ranking (officers' requests often take precedence over those of enlisted persons).

Sequel: What next? This word, pronounced SEEK-wull, is based on *sequ*, from the Latin "to follow." A sequel follows something similar that came before. Many books and movies (like the original *Star Wars*) are followed by sequels.

Related words: *Sequence, sequential.* There's also the term *prequel* (a coined word not often used in formal English), which means the original that the sequel was based on.

Fin de Siecle: This French phrase literally means *end of the century*. It was originally applied to the last years of the 19th century, and suggested a time of progressive ideas and customs (with some suggestion of decadence and loose morals). But some people applied it to the period around the end of the 20th century, and many would say that the definition still holds.

It can be used as a noun (They lived during the *fin de siecle*) or an adjective (those *fin de siecle* parties were really something).

It's not easy to pronounce this French mouthful, but a close approximation is fahn-duh-see-ACHE-luh.

Millennium: This word literally means 1,000 years (Latin *mil*, thousand; and *annus* or *ennium*, year). So in 2001, we began a new millenium. It also means any period of great happiness, peace, and prosperity.

Exercise 2 – A: It's About Time

> **Directions:** In each item below, you'll find two terms, separated by a virgule (/), that are related in some way (e.g., long/short). A third ("single") term is separated by a virgule from a series of terms in parentheses. For each item, circle the term in parentheses that has *the same relationship* to the "single" term as the paired terms have to each other.

1. ocean/aquatic = stars/ *(solar, terrestrial, martian, sidereal)*

2. century/hundred = millennium/ *(billion, million, thousand, hundred)*

3. nocturnal/ *(hawks, robins, owls, buzzards)* = diurnal/cows

4. *(delay, hurry, ignore, refuse)* procrastinate = reply/answer

5. precedent/go before = *(ancestor, duplicate, contemporary, sequel)*/follow

6. diurnal/day = crepuscular/ *(morning, noon, twilight, midnight)*

7. midday/noon = *(contemporary, prior, sequential, antedating)*/concurrent

8. anachronism/timely = zoo/ *(panda, elephant, dinosaur, rhinoceros)*

9. last class/school day = fin de siecle/ *(semester, year, decade, century)*

10. abreast/side-by-side = synchronous/ *(faster, slower, at the same time, at different times)*

Exercise 2 – B: It's About Time

Directions: Write a letter in each blank, matching the words in the first column with the clues in the second column.

Words

_____ 1. anachronistic

_____ 2. diurnal

_____ 3. sequel

_____ 4. synchronous

_____ 5. fin de siecle

_____ 6. crepuscular

_____ 7. precedent

_____ 8. procrastinate

_____ 9. sidereal

_____10. nocturnal

Clues

a. owls and bats

b. Rocky II

c. previous case

d. can it wait?

e. twilight time

f. daily

g. by the stars

h. in the 90's

i. wrong time

j. same time

Exercise 2 – C: Write the Word

1. My motto is "Never do today what you can put off until tomorrow."
   I'm a/an _____.

2. Something that's out of place in time is called _____.

3. Here's a word that describes things (or people) who like to prowl at
   night. It's _____.

4. When books or movies make a lot of money, the publishers or
   producers usually rush to get out a follow-on version. This
   second-generation production is called a/an _____.

5. This phrase, taken from another language, means "end of the century."
   It's _____.

6. This word refers to things that happen daily — like sunrise or sunset.
   It's _____.

7. A spaceship in a cowboy movie would be a/an _____.

8. If you're meeting someone at a specified time, you want to make sure
   your watches are showing the same time. The word for watches (or
   events) running or occurring at the same time is _____.

9. This word means *something that happened before*, and it often refers to
   a legal decision. The word is _____.

10. Some animals are active at night, some during the day. But others
    prefer the gray areas between daylight and dark. They're

    _____.

Unit 3 – About Money

Two friends were reading a newspaper story about a big lottery winner. "Well," said one, "money isn't everything."

"Maybe not," the other replied, "but it's way ahead of whatever's in second place."

That little joke reflects common attitudes about money. No matter how we may feel about it personally, we have to admit that it's important to almost everyone.

We have a wide range of financial conditions in this country — from abject poverty to multibillion-dollar wealth. And we also have a broad range of attitudes toward money. Some people want to get all they can, and to keep it as long as they can. Others seem less concerned about money, and some people want to spend it as soon as they get it.

The words in this unit will help us put labels on the haves and the have-nots. We'll learn terms that indicate how wealthy (or poor) someone is, and also words to describe some different attitudes about money.

Affluent: (AFF-lu-unt or af-FLU-unt) It's hard to say exactly where the line is that separates the rich from the poor. But wherever it is, the affluent person is on the side we'd all like to be on. The person who lives in affluence is rich — but just *how* rich? After all, there's barely rich, and there's really rich, and there's super-rich.

In most people's plain English, the affluent person is not close to the top, but is comfortably rich. The typical affluent person, if there is such a thing, might own a very large house in a good neighborhood, another home (or two) for getaways and vacations, a couple of nice cars, and maybe a comfortable boat.

Opulent: There's a true story about a very rich man who had ordered a huge, custom-built yacht. When his friend (not quite as rich) asked about the price of buying and operating such a vessel, he replied "If you have to ask, you can't afford it."

That's an example of the super-rich talking to the merely very rich. If we envy those who are richer than we are, then affluent people may well look with envy on those who live in opulence (OP-you-lunce). The opulent (OP-you-lunt) person doesn't have to ask the price of anything. Instead of a luxury yacht, such a person might own a shipyard. Instead of a private plane, there'd be a fleet, with full-time pilots and mechanics. Instead of membership in a good country club, this person might own a club. Or two or three or more.

Destitute: Okay, back to reality, where there's poverty too. While there are many affluent people in our society, and even a few opulent ones, there are also many who are destitute (DESS-tuh-tute). These people don't worry about a luxury car, or a second car. They don't even have a car — and maybe not even a second-hand bicycle.

People who live in destitution not only don't have life's luxuries, they don't even have the necessities. They don't have enough money to adequately feed and clothe their families, to pay for medical treatment, or for the other daily needs that most of use take more or less for granted.

The word sounds a little like *desperate*, and that's not too far off. Destitute people are poor people, often desperately poor.

Frugal: Now let's shift from how much money people have, and look at their *attitudes* toward money. You probably know someone who pinches every penny, watches every expense, hates to spend money. Such people could be called *stingy* or *miserly*. Fortunately, such people are rare.

Move up a notch on the loosening-up scale, and you have the person who is not stingy, but who's, well, *careful* about money. The kind of person who keeps a budget, follows it religiously, always shops for the best prices, saves regularly. The person may be likeable, and is not afraid to spend money — as long it's for a good reason.

Such people are *frugal* (FROO-gul). And they practice frugality (froo-GAL-uh-tee). This doesn't mean that they're bad folks. In fact, there's a lot to be said for them. They pay their debts, and have something put aside so they can handle an emergency. They're careful with money, and many of us sometimes wish we could be a little more frugal.

Parsimonious: Frugal folks are okay — we can understand them. But parsimonious (par-suh-MOAN-ee-us) people are just too careful with their money. In fact, they're downright stingy. Their parsimony (PAR-suh-mony), or over-concern with money, keeps them from being much fun at all.

Avaricious: If your frugal friends sometimes get on your nerves, you'll really dislike avaricious (av-ur-ISH-ous) people. Why? Because they not only want to keep all the money they have, but they also want to get yours, too. Avarice (AV-ur-us) is extreme greed, a constant desire for more wealth, no matter how much is already possessed.

Profligate: We've talked about frugal people, and a little about parsimonious ones as well. On the other end of the attitudinal scale are those people who seem eager to throw money away — whether they have it or not.

The profligate (PROF-luh-gut) person is wasteful, even recklessly extravagant with money. Unless the profligate person happens also to be opulent, the money will soon be gone. And if more comes in, it will be gone too. Frugality is not in the profligate person's vocabulary. Money is easy come, easy go. There's no watching expenditures, no hesitation about spending all the money that's available.

Philanthropist: Here's the kind of person we'd like to be — at least in terms of wealth and attitude toward money. The roots that make up this word give us a good clue to its meaning. The combining form *phil* means *love,* and *anthropo* means *people.* The philanthropist loves people — and shows it.

And that showing is what makes it impossible for most of us to become known as philanthropists, no matter how much we love people. To earn the label, you'd have to have a lot of money — a whole lot — and you'd have to give it away, in bundles (usually to charities or to what people consider good causes). So there are two requirements for being a philanthropist (fuh-LAN-thruh-pist). One is to have lots of money, and the other is to give a lot of it away.

Penurious: This word (pen-YOUR-ee-us) has two definitions, related but different. The older one means really stingy or miserly. The newer definition is *living in extreme poverty*. Or you could use the noun form, and say living in penury (PEN-you-ree). The second definition, super-poor, is the one most likely intended when the word is used these days. But a little of the flavor of stinginess still hangs onto the word, so you would not be likely to use it for good-hearted or generous people, no matter how poor they are.

Fiscal: This is a plain, unexciting little word. It simply means *financial*, or having something to do with money. It's often used in news stories about government policies on taxing and spending.

It's included here for two reasons. The first is that it's so commonly used that we should know it. The second is that it's often mispronounced. The standard pronunciation is FISS-kul, with only two syllables. But some people mistakenly pronounce it the same way we say the word *physical*, with three syllables. So be frugal — save a syllable.

Lucre: Here's another word that has changed over the years. When this word was used in centuries past, it simply meant *money* or *riches*. But the term has somehow lost its reputation and status, and nobody uses it seriously anymore. It's mainly used in a humorous, derogatory sense, as in "I am a professional athlete (or entertainer or politician) not because of the money, but because I love what I'm doing. You don't think I'm in it just for the filthy lucre, do you?" It's pronounced LOO-kur.

Exercise 3 – A: About Money

> **Directions:** In each item below, you'll find two terms, separated by a virgule (/), that are related in some way (e.g., long/short). A third ("single") term is separated by a virgule from a series of terms in parentheses. For each item, circle the term in parentheses that has *the same relationship* to the "single" term as the paired terms have to each other.

1. daredevil/careful = big-spender/ *(miserly, stingy, frugal, parsimonious)*

2. wealthy/ *(affluent, opulent, fiscal, destitute)* = rich/poor

3. *(philatelist, philanderer, philanthropist, philodendron)*/miser = generous/stingy

4. pauper/king = poverty/ *(destitution, frugality, penury, opulence)*

5. wealth/ *(poverty, affluence, penury, bankruptcy)* = damp/moist

6. exercise/physical = budgeting/ *(fiscal, partial, actual, continual)*

7. *(credit card, bankbook, lucre, ledger)*/money = car/automobile

8. impoverished/ *(affluent, penurious, opulent, wealthy)* = dry/arid

9. rapid/speedy = wasteful/ *(profitable, promiscuous, promising, profligate)*

10. thought/idea = *(avarice, generosity, philanthropy, frugality)*/greed

Exercise 3 – B: About Money

Directions: Write a letter in each blank, matching the words in the first column with the clues in the second column.

Words	Clues
____ 1. lucre	a. rich as a king
____ 2. avarice	b. rich, but not super-rich
____ 3. affluent	c. stingy, or poor
____ 4. destitute	d. about money
____ 5. fiscal	e. careful with money
____ 6. penurious	f. greed
____ 7. frugal	g. free-spender
____ 8. profligate	h. poor as a church mouse
____ 9. philanthropist	i. money
____ 10. opulent	j. gives big money to good causes

Exercise 3 – C: Write the Word

1. I'm not stingy, but I *am* careful with my money. I don't like to waste any, and I keep pretty close track of where each dollar goes.
   I'm _____.

2. This guy's more than careful with money, he's downright stingy. He's so tight that he watches every penny, and really hates to part with one.
   He's _____.

3. She's not just rich, she's super-rich. If she decides to fly somewhere for a vacation, she won't make plane reservations, she'll have her pilot bring her private jet around. And probably fly to one of her lavish homes in exotic places. She's _____.

4. Talk about broke, I'm so broke I can't even pay attention. Not only can I not afford new clothes, I can't afford to buy *old* clothes from the second-hand store. Never mind luxuries, I don't even have enough money for the necessities of life. I'm _____.

5. Some people are generous, some are a little tight. This guy not only wants to keep all his own money, he wants to get *yours*, too. He's more than greedy, he's _____.

6. Not me, buddy. Money is just so much green paper until it's used to buy things. So I spend it, as fast as I can get it. You could say I'm reckless with money, or that I'm _____.

7. I guess you could call me an altruist with lots of money. Because I have
   a lot, I think it's good to help others. So I give a lot of money
   away — to charities and other good causes. I'm a/an

   _____.

8. This term is used to describe people who are really poor, but the word
   also suggests that they're stingy. They're

   _____.

9. This word may seem a little bureaucratic, and it's often used by
   government agencies and banks and such. It simply means having to
   do with money or funding. The word is _____.

10. I'm rich, but I'm not *super-rich*, like that lucky lady up there in
    number three. I've got a second luxury car, a good boat, a country
    home. But I'm not rich enough to have my own plane or private island
    or a couple of big mansions that I keep fully staffed. Like a lot of
    successful professionals, I'm simply _____.

Unit 4 – Health Practitioners

In the old days, when we were sick we went to "the doctor." Most physicians were family doctors, expected to treat all kinds of illnesses, in people of all ages. They wrote prescriptions, delivered babies, performed surgery, set bones, told us what to eat and what to avoid. With such a broad range of responsibilities, it's no wonder they were known as GP's (for *general practitioners*). The GP (almost always a man) was expected to take care of us, no matter what our health problems were.

But in the last few decades, medical researchers have learned a lot more about our health and our bodies than those GP's could possibly know. This scientific knowledge has grown much too rapidly for any one person to keep up with it.

The result has been specialization — physicians and other health practitioners limiting their practices to one particular part of the body or one aspect of medicine. Sometimes it's hard to keep the names of these specialists straight; this unit will help.

Optometrist: From *opto* (eye) and *meter* (measure), this specialist is highly trained and certified, but is probably not an M.D. The *optometrist* (op-TOM-uh-trist) measures vision and prescribes glasses, but does not perform surgery or treat eye diseases.

Optician: The *optician* (also from *opto*) is a skilled craftsperson who grinds lenses and makes glasses, but does not measure vision or practice medicine. The word's pronounced op-TISH-un.

Oculist/Ophthalmologist: The *oculist* (OCK-you-list) is an M.D., a fully certified physician who may perform surgery, prescribe medicine, and otherwise treat patients who have eye problems. *Ophthalmologist* (auf-thal-MOLL-uh-jist) is just a fancier word for the same doctor.

Gynecologist: *Gyn* means **woman**, and the *gynecologist* specializes in women's diseases and conditions. How to pronounce it?

GUY-nuh-coll-uh-jist is probably most common, but it's hard to go wrong, because it's okay to say GIN-uh-coll-uh-jist, or even JINE-uh-coll-uh-jist.

Pediatrician: The spelling of this one could be a little misleading, because *ped* sometimes means *foot* (as in *pedal*). But *pediatrician* comes from *paidos*, which means *child* — the pediatrician (pee-dee-uh-TRISH-un) treats children. (A foot doctor is called a *podiatrist*.)

Dermatologist: *Derm* means *skin*, as in *epidermis* and *pachyderm*. And *dermatitis* is one of the many conditions this skin specialist treats. This doctor is called a durm-uh-TOL-uh-jist.

Cardiologist: The root *card* means *heart*. The cardiologist (card-ee-OLL-uh-jist) is a doctor who specializes in this vital organ, and who may give you an *electocardiogram* (often called an E-K-G), may treat *tachycardia* (too-rapid heartbeat), or may check the *pericardial* sac around your heart.

Internist: Of all the folks we've looked at, this one is closest to the old general practitioner (who didn't specialize). This doctor does specialize, in a way. But not in any given part of the body or health condition. Instead, the field of specialization here is *diagnosis.* This doctor very often does tests and examinations to find out what's wrong, then refers the patient to a specialist in treating that condition.

Neurologist: This physician specializes in the nervous system — the complex network of nerves that extends from the brain throughout the body. The term neurologist (nyoor-OL-uh-jist) comes from *neuro,* which means *nerve.*

Psychiatrist: An M.D., this practitioner can prescribe medicines and may perform surgery. But as the name suggests (*psyche* means *mind*), the psychiatrist (sigh-KYE-uh-trist) specializes in mental, emotional, or behavioral disorders. (The slang term for this doctor is *shrink*.)

Pedodontist: This word combines *ped* (meaning *child*, as in pediatrician) with *dont* (teeth), so a pedodontist (ped-uh-DON-tist) specializes in children's dentistry.

Orthodontist: *Ortho* means *straight* or *straighten*. The orthodontist (orth-uh-DON-tist) is a dentist who specializes in fitting braces and straightening teeth.

Obstetrician: Pregnancy and childbirth are the concerns of the *obstetrician* (ob-stuh-TRISH-un). Many of these physicians have a double speciality — one in obstetrics, the other in gynecology. That's where the term "OB–GYN" comes from.

Exercise 4 – A: Health Practitioners

> **Directions:** In each item below, you'll find two terms, separated by a virgule (/), that are related in some way (e.g., long/short). A third ("single") term is separated by a virgule from a series of terms in parentheses. For each item, circle the term in parentheses that has *the same relationship* to the "single" term as the paired terms have to each other.

1. mechanic/automobile = oculist/ *(feet, skin, eyes, heart)*

2. woman/ *(gynecologist, podiatrist, cardiologist, ophthalmologist)* = child/pediatrician

3. apple peel/apple core = *(cardiologist, optician, psychiatrist, dermatologist)*/surgeon

4. *(dermatologist, optician, cardiologist, podiatrist)*/ophthalmologist = seamstress/dress-designer

5. optometrist/ *(blood-pressure, muscle-strength, vision, height)* = scales/weight

6. *(children, women, old-timers, mine-workers)*/pediatrician = pets/veterinarian

7. landscaper/lawns = *(podiatrist, pediatrician, cardiologist, neurologist)*/nerves

8. flat-fixer/wheel aligner = cavity-filler/ *(optician, orthodontist, podiatrist, cardiologist)*

9. cardiologist/ *(feet, teeth, eyes, heart)* = financial advisor/money

10. emotional illness/psychiatrist = *(insomnia, listlessness, pregnancy, infancy)*/obstetrician

Exercise 4 – B: Health Practitioners

Directions: Write a letter in each blank, matching the terms in the first column with the clues in the second column.

Terms

_____ 1. optometrist

_____ 2. optician

_____ 3. oculist

_____ 4. ophthalmologist

_____ 5. gynecologist

_____ 6. pediatrician

_____ 7. dermatologist

_____ 8. cardiologist

_____ 9. neurologist

_____ 10. psychiatrist

_____ 11. pedodontist

_____ 12. orthodontist

_____ 13. obstetrician

_____ 14. internist

_____ 15. podiatrist

Clues

a. women's doctor

b. skin doctor

c. a shrink

d. kids' teeth

e. grinds lenses

f. kids' doctor

g. delivers babies

h. measures vision

i. diagnoses illnesses

j. treats nerves

k. eye doctor

l. foot doctor

m. heart specialist

n. tooth straightener

o. fancy "oculist"

Exercise 4 – C: Health Practitioners

> **Directions:** Write each practitioner's specialty in the blank.

Who?	Specializes in What
Example: otologist	*ear*
1. internist	
2. gynecologist	
3. obstetrician	
4. pediatrician	
5. dermatologist	
6. ophthalmologist	
7. cardiologist	
8. neurologist	
9. psychiatrist	
10. podiatrist	
11. orthodontist	
12. optometrist	
13. optician	
14. oculist	
15. pedodontist	

Exercise 4 – D: Write the Word

1. She's a physician who specializes in women's health problems and conditions. She's a/an _____.

2. This is the doctor you'd go to if you have a skin problem — like acne, psoriasis, or eczema. He's a/an _____.

3. Do you need glasses (or a change of prescription)? She may not be an M.D., but she's trained to measure your vision and to prescribe glasses. She's a/an _____.

4. So you have a prescription, and this guy's going to grind the lenses and make the glasses to fill it. He's a/an_____.

5. If you need an M.D. for eye surgery or such, the person you'd see is a/an _____.

6. She's a heart specialist, called a/an _____.

7. This physician specializes in caring for women during their pregnancy and childbirth. He's a/an _____.

8. After a few years, you may need to see a doctor who specializes in children's dentistry. He's a/an _____.

9. If the kid needs braces, you'd make an appointment with a/an _____, who specializes in straightening teeth.

10. If the stress really gets to us, and we're afraid of losing our mental grip on reality, we could go see a *shrink*, or _____.

Unit 5 – Who's in Charge Here?

Get a group of people together, and they're almost sure to organize themselves into some kind of power structure. But what kind will it be? Do they give complete, life-or-death power to a king or emperor? Or do the people keep the power themselves, making decisions as a group of equals? Humans have tried both methods, as well as just about everything in between. The results have ranged from great to awful.

In this unit, we'll look at some of the words for the most common forms of government, and touch on a few related terms as well.

Democracy: This word (pronounced duh-MOCK-ruh-see) comes from the Greek roots *demos* (people), and *kratein* (rule). It literally means government by all the people, but there are not many pure democracies. In the U.S., for example, we elect people to represent us in lawmaking groups such as the Congress.

Republic: In a republic (like the U.S.), the ultimate power rests in all the citizens entitled to vote. But the citizens entrust this power to elected representatives, who are supposed to act for their constituents — the people who elected them. (It's pronounced ree-PUB-lick.)

Aristocracy: This word (pronounced arris-TOCK-ruh-see) literally means rule by the most capable (Greek *aristos*, best). But in actual practice, it often means government by a privileged minority or upper class (the aristocracy).

Plutocracy: The Greek term *ploutos* means *wealth*, so *plutocracy* means government by the rich. As commonly used in our country, it applies not so much to the official government as to the behind-the-scenes influence the very rich have on our lawmakers and government executives. (It's pronounced plu-TOCK-ruh-see.)

Oligarchy: This term (pronounced O-luh-garky), often applied to a business or social organization as well as to government, means rule by a few people (Greek *oligo*, few) who have managed to gain and retain power.

Nepotism: Some skeptics say "It's not *what* you know, but *who* you know." We often hear such comments after a person of questionable ability gets a plum promotion, or is appointed to a position of power, prestige, or wealth. And we're much more likely to hear griping if the person happens to be a relative of whoever made the appointment. The practice of putting relatives into desirable positions, sometimes positions of great power, is called *nepotism* (NEP-uh-tism). The word comes from a Latin word meaning *grandson* or *nephew*.

Meritocracy: In some groups, power goes to the rich, or the strong, or the ones who get the most votes. But in a *meritocracy* (mer-uh-TOCK-ruh-see), positions of leadership go to those who have the most brains — or at least appear to be the brightest and the best. As you might guess, this doesn't usually happen in actual governments — at the state, local, or national levels. We're most likely to find meritocracies in institutions such as universities, think tanks, or associations dealing with arts and sciences.

Monarchy: The Greek *mono* means one or alone, so monarchy literally means rule by only one person. But in the modern world, the monarch's powers are often limited and shared by the people through their representatives. The two common varieties of monarchy (MON-are-kee) are *absolute* (unlimited) and *constitutional* (curtailed or limited).

Militocracy: As you'd guess, this word means rule by the military. It often follows a *coup d'état*, a forcible takeover of government. *Militocracy* is not a common word (it's absent from some good dictionaries), but seems likely to become established. It's pronounced mill-uh-TOCK-ruh-see.

Theocracy: The term theocracy (thee-OCK-ruh-see) comes from the Greek root *the*, which means *god*. So a literal meaning would be rule by a god, or the gods. But in practice, it usually means that the government is run by a church, or its representatives. In some theocratic societies, the rulers claim to be agents of a god, ruling with divine approval and authority.

Kakistocracy: When politics becomes so dirty that good people want nothing to do with it, there's always the danger that power will be grabbed up by the people who hunger for it most, but deserve it least. If we let this go too far, we could wind up with a *kakistocracy*, or rule by the very worst people (from Greek *kakos*, bad). The root is found in cacophony (kuh-KOFF-uh-knee), meaning "harsh sounding."

Interregnum: This word originally meant the period between two successive reigns (the time between the death of a king and the coronation of the new king is an *interregnum*). It now means any period when the normal functions of government or management are suspended or greatly diminished. It is sometimes used in referring to the transition period between the election of a new president and the inauguration.

Anarchy: "That government is best which governs least," it's been said. If you carry this idea to its illogical conclusion, then the very best form of government would be *anarchy*, or no government at all. For obvious reasons, the term is often applied to situations of chaos or disorder. (It's pronounced ANN-ark-ee.)

Ochlocracy: We complain about our government sometimes. But most of us would have to admit that it's better than anarchy, or no government at all. One danger of anarchy is that it may lead to a situation even worse and more dangerous. When nobody seems to be in charge, angry mobs may take to the streets, and take control. Such mob rule is called *ochlocracy* (ock-LOCK-ruh-see) from the Greek *ochlos*, a mob.

Exercise 5 – A: Who's in Charge?

> **Directions:** Match the words in the first column with the clues in the second column.

Word

Clue

_____ 1. plutocracy

a. a privileged upper class

_____ 2. democracy

b. a few cronies (the "in crowd")

_____ 3. aristocracy

c. the worst people

_____ 4. republic

d. leaders and their relatives

_____ 5. oligarchy

e. academic overachievers

_____ 6. meritocracy

f. mobs

_____ 7. monarchy

g. the very rich

_____ 8. militocracy

h. one absolute ruler

_____ 9. theocracy

i. the uniformed brass

_____10. kakistocracy

j. representatives of the people

_____11. interregnum

k. the time between regimes

_____12. anarchy

l. nobody at all

_____13. ochlocracy

m. the people themselves

_____14. nepotism

n. religious leaders

Exercise 5 – B: Who's in Charge?

Directions: In each item below, you'll find two terms, separated by a virgule (/), that are related in some way (e.g., long/short). A third ("single") term is separated by a virgule from a series of terms in parentheses. For each item, circle the term in parentheses that has *the same relationship* to the "single" term as the paired terms have to each other.

1. baseball/umpires = democracy/ *(bureaucrats, a few, the people, the rich)*

2. republic/ *(representatives, military, the people, no one)* = traffic/cops

3. leader/band = *(military, mobs, bureaucrats, church)*/theocracy

4. *(senator, king, lobbyist, president)*/monarchy = stallion/herd

5. class/teacher = kakistocracy/ *(best, worst, most, least)*

6. quarterback/football team = *(men, women, rich, poor)* /plutocracy

7. meritocracy/ *(army, business, mob, university)* = monarchy/kingdom

8. *(nobody, everybody, a few, the elite)*/anarchy = majority/club

9. army/top brass = nepotism/ *(mobs, kinfolk, preachers, kings)*

10. mobs/ *(ochlocracy, militocracy, democracy, plutocracy)* = toughest wolf/pack

Exercise 5 – C: Write the Word

1. Government of the people, for the people, and by the people — that's a basic principle of this country. When the people run their governments directly (as they do in some town meetings where anyone who lives there can come out and vote on issues), it's called a/an

   _____.

2. Of course, it's hard to have all the people deciding every little thing. That's why we elect others to represent us in Congress. The U.S. national government is called a/an _____.

3. Some people say that the rich people really control things from behind the scenes, using their money to make sure votes go the way they want. A government controlled by the very rich is called a/an

   _____.

4. Some of us don't trust politicians, and would like for more good people to get into office. The practice of putting people into positions of authority because they have earned it, because they deserve it, is called a/an _____.

5. In some places (such as the Vatican), church leaders are in control of government. Such an arrangement is called a/an

   _____.

6. In some countries, especially those with unstable governments, a group of army officers may take control of the government by force (this is called staging a coup). The new government, run by the officers, is called a/an _____.

7. Sometimes a ruler may be assassinated, or leave the country in fear, so that *nobody* is in charge of the government. Such a condition is called

    _____.

8. If nobody comes in to take control, people may form into mobs who more or less rule things. Such mob-rule is called

    _____.

9. In some governments, organizations, and businesses, people put their kinfolk into positions of authority. This practice is called

    _____.

10. We've had words for government by all people, government by officers, by the church, by mobs, and by the best people. But here's a word that means government *by the worst people*. The word is

    _____.

Unit 6 – Sciences and Pseudosciences

Science comes from a Latin root meaning *to know*. So a science is a body of knowledge about a subject. The suffix *ist* means *one who,* so a scientist is one who learns about a subject, one who comes to *know* a lot about it. And the combining form *pseudo* means *false.* (It's pronounced SUE-dough.) A pseudointellectual is a person who pretends to be an intellectual, and a pseudoscience is not widely considered a true science. The following words apply to some of the best-known scientists and pseudoscientists.

Anthropologist: This scientist studies human beings — their physical characteristics, their customs, languages, and how they spread out around the world. The root *anthropos* means *mankind.* You'll find it in words like *misanthrope, philanthropist,* and many others.

A related and slightly overlapping term is *archaeologist,* applied to a person who specializes in the study of ancient groups of people. These are the scientists who go out on "digs," methodically unearthing bones, pottery shards, and anything else they can find in the sites of ancient villages and other dwelling sites.

Astronomer: *Astro* means *star,* but that's not all this scientist studies. Astronomy also includes the study of just about everything out in space — planets, asteroids, radio waves, black holes, and lots of other exciting things now being discovered.

Astrologer: Astrologer use historical charts showing the positions of the planets at the time of a person's birth to analyze personality traits and life events. Astrology is considered a pseudoscience, but many people consult their horoscopes, hoping to learn something that will help them.

Geologist: That root *geo* means *earth,* so the geologist is literally someone who studies our planet. This scientist is interested in earth forms (such as different kinds of rocks, oil deposits), in how the earth was formed, and in the different parts, from the molten middle to the outer crust.

Volcanologist: (Sometimes spelled *vulcanologist*) This scientist is a specialist in one area of geology — volcanoes. The speciality is pronounced vol-kun-OL-uh-gee, and it deals with formation, eruptions, and predictions of volcanic activity. A lot of progress has been made in this science, but we still can't be sure when or where the next volcano will pop up or erupt.

Phrenologist: We have another pseudoscience here. People involved in phrenology (fruh-NOLL-uh-gee) claimed to be able to tell what's *inside* a person's head by feeling the bumps and shapes on the *outside*. This claim has mostly been rejected as nonsense, but people used to take their children to phrenologists to find out about their talents, intelligence, and career options.

Biologist: Don't let that *bi* at the beginning fool you into thinking this word has to do with the study of *two* somethings. The prefix here is *bio*, which means *life*. So this scientist studies all living things. This is a broad field, so it is divided into such specializations as *zoology* and *botany*, which are themselves subdivided into many smaller areas of study.

Graphologist: This term sort of spills over the line between science and pseudoscience. Many years ago, some people claimed to be able to tell us about a person's character, skills, and other personal and psychological attributes by analyzing that person's handwriting. Although those claims have been widely rejected, the term *graphologist* is sometimes used in reference to some perfectly legitimate people. These folks are handwriting experts. They may not be able to tell a person's character or talents, but they can be very helpful in criminal cases, providing expert opinions about handwriting — whether a signature is authentic or a forgery, for example.

Zoologist: The *zoo* is a combining form meaning *animal,* and that's the field of study here. The pronunciation can be a little tricky, because the two *o*'s are separated into two syllables. We say zoe-OL-uh-jist. (The first syllable rhymes with *toe.*) This is a branch of biology, of course, and it deals with animal life rather than vegetable life.

Botanist: This word comes from a Greek root meaning *plant,* and that's what the botanist studies. The science of botany (commonly pronounced about like BOTT-knee) is the branch of biology that deals with plant life. Like zoology, it's subdivided into many smaller areas of study.

Entomologist: We said that the science of zoology is subdivided, and this is one of the divisions. Entomologists (en-tuh-MOLL-uh-jists) study insects — six-legged creatures. The entomologist's interest ranges from army ants to killer bees and many, many other insects, both helpful and harmful.

Speleologist: This scientist spends a good deal of time underground, because speleology (spee-lee-OL-uh-gee) is the study and exploration of caves.

Exercise 6 – A: Sciences and Pseudosciences

> **Directions:** In each item below, you'll find two terms, separated by a virgule (/), that are related in some way (e.g., long/short). A third ("single") term is separated by a virgule from a series of terms in parentheses. For each item, circle the term in parentheses that has *the same relationship* to the "single" term as the paired terms have to each other.

1. anthropologist/ *(caves, minerals, stars, people)* = spectator/sports

2. astronomer/telescope = astrologer/
   (microscope, horoscope, periscope, stethoscope)

3. botanist/phrenologist = *(plants, ants, spiders, insects)*/bumps

4. miner/mine = speleologist/ *(nave, wave, cave, grave)*

5. *(caves, stars, bones, music)*/archeologist = gold/miner

6. graphologist/ *(tarot cards, head-bumps, palms, handwriting)* =
   fortune-teller/crystal ball

7. *(tides, lava, birds, fish)*/vulcanologist = animal tracks/hunter

8. subjects/students = *(living things, minerals, heavenly bodies, stamps)*/
   biologists

9. zoologist/ *(rose, solar eclipse, oak tree, giraffe)* = bird-watcher/eagle

10. bird-watcher/birds = entomologist/ *(bats, birds, insects, spiders)*

Exercise 6 – B: Write the Word

1. You don't need expensive tests to find out about your kids' IQ and talents. I'll do it on the cheap, just by feeling the bumps on their heads. I'm a/an _____.

2. I study the stars, trying to discover new ones. I also want to find out more about such strange things as black holes. I'm a serious scientist, and my branch of science is called _____.

3. My interest is not on the heavens, but on the earth. I study our planet and things that make it up — rocks, oil deposits, shifts of the earth's crust. I'm a/an _____.

4. I'm also interested in our world, but my focus is on plants and animals that live on our planet. I'm a/an _____.

5. I'm also a scientist who studies living things. But I'm not into plants (except in my garden or salad). Animal life is what my branch of science is about, so I'm called a/an _____.

6. Not me. Animals are okay, but I'm more interested in plants, and that's what scientists in my field study. I'm a/an

   _____.

7. Me, I'm into insects. Those little six-legged creatures are important in many ways, so that's what I study. I'm called a/an

   _____.

8. I'm not recognized as a legitimate scientist, but many people read my books and newspaper columns. I tell people how the stars and planets will affect their lives. I'm a/an _____.

9. I don't believe you can tell much about people by what's happening in the skies, or by feeling the bumps on their heads. Let me look at their handwriting, and I'll tell you some of their deepest secrets. I'm a/an

_____.

10. I don't waste time on bugs, or plants, or what's happening in the skies. I'm interested in *us* — the people who live on this planet. I'm a/an

_____.

Exercise 6 – C: Sciences and Pseudosciences

Directions: Fill in the blanks.

Who?   **Studies What?**

1. anthropologist

2. astronomer

3. geologist

4. volcanologist

5. phrenologist

6. biologist

7. astrologer

8. graphologist

9. zoologist

10. botanist

11. entomologist

Unit 7 – Words About Words

It's been said that speech is silver, but silence is golden. In this section, we'll look at some words to describe people who talk a lot, and people who talk little. And you may find a word or two about yourself. (Does *articulate* fit?)

Verbose: The term *verb* comes from a Latin term meaning *word*. The *verbose* person uses lots of words, never seeming to say anything briefly. Of course, sometimes a lot of words are needed to get a complex idea across. But the term verbose (vur-BOSE) suggests that more words are being used than are really needed. The word may apply to things as well as people — a speech, letter, or memo can be verbose. The noun form is *verbosity* (vur-BOS-uh-tee).

Garrulous: Here's another word about someone who talks a lot. *Garrulous* is a lot like *verbose*, but there's a subtle difference. A verbose person may have something important to say, but uses too many words to say it. But calling a person garrulous (GARE-uh-lus) implies that the person is a chatterbox or gossip, talking almost constantly, usually about unimportant things. We may enjoy listening to a verbose friend, but the conversation of a garrulous person is almost always *vapid* (VAP-id) or *banal* (BAY-nul) — which means it's uninteresting, flat, boring.

Laconic: Verbose and garrulous people talk a lot. On the other hand, there are people who don't talk very much at all. The *laconic* (luh-CON-ik) person may listen intently, but seem disinclined toward talk for the sake of talking. So, when the laconic person does have something to say, it's usually short and to the point. "Silent Cal" Coolidge is a good example. A young reporter sitting next to Coolidge at a dinner told him that she had bet her editor that she could get her dinner partner to say more than two words during the meal. "You lose," was his laconic reply.

Logorrhea: Compared to the person with *logorrhea*, the verbose person seems quiet. Did you ever know somebody who never seemed to stop talking? Someone whose mouth just seemed to produce a continuous string of words — a gushing, never-ending flow? A good term to describe this river of words is *logorrhea* (log-uh-REE-uh). It comes from *logo* (meaning *word*) and *rrhea* (*flow*). So if you know someone who's a gusher-mouth, you can say that the person suffers from logorrhea.

Articulate: Skill in anything is admirable, and the *articulate* (are-TICK-you-lut) person has admirable skill with words. Where you and I may have a thought that's difficult to put into words, the articulate person seems able to roll out the perfect sentence, the exact combination of words needed to express an idea. The person's speech is neither too much nor too little, but just the right amount— just the right words. The verb form, spelled the same way, is pronounced are-TICK-you-late. So the articulate speaker is one who can articulate ideas fluently, clearly, and cogently.

Verbiage: The words that the *verbose* person uses to fill the page or speech are referred to as *verbiage* (VURB-ee-ij). Some people use the term as a synonym for any kind of words, but more-careful writers and speakers realize that it usually connotes a superfluity or plethora of words — it implies that there are just too many of them. For example: *this is not a bad letter, if we can cut out some of the verbiage and get to the point quicker.*

Cogent: The word *cogent* (KO-junt) is commonly used to describe speech, rather than the speaker. *Cogent* speech is marked by clarity, precision, and intelligence. A cogent answer is more than satisfactory— it leaves no doubt that the speaker fully understands the question, and it shows insight and wit. We admire and appreciate *cogency* (KO-jun-cee).

Euphemism: To avoid using terms that may be considered offensive or pejorative, we often resort to a milder word. Such a substitute term is called a *euphemism* (YOU-fuh-miz'm). *Passed away* (for "died") is a common example. Others are *revenue enhancement* (for "taxes"), *misspoke* (for "lied"), and *eccentric* (for "weird" or "nutty"). A person who uses lots of euphemisms is indulging in one kind of *circumlocution*— talking around the issue, without getting directly to the point. Politicians may come to mind.

Colloquial: This word is often misunderstood to mean something like "used almost exclusively in a certain geographical area." But as used by careful speakers and writers, it means "used in informal, everyday conversation, but not in writing or formal speech." *Colloquial* (kuh-LOW-kwee-ul) usually refers to spoken language, but is sometimes used in reference to informal writing as well (such as a note or letter to a close friend or family member). Note: a better word for an expression used primarily in a certain area is *sectionalism* or *regionalism*.

Pejorative: A useful term, *pejorative* (pee-JORE-uh-tive) means having a distinctly unfavorable connotation — maybe even somewhat insulting. Most of the words used as racial or ethnic slurs are *pejorative* terms. You can always say that you didn't intend to use a word in its *pejorative* sense, but once you've used it, you almost always have a tough time explaining it away.

Exercise 7 – A: Words About Words

Directions: In each item below, you'll find two terms, separated by a virgule (/), that are related in some way (e.g., long/short). A third ("single") term is separated by a virgule from a series of terms in parentheses. For each item, circle the term in parentheses that has *the same relationship* to the "single" term as the paired terms have to each other.

1. extroverted/shy = verbose/ *(loud, quiet, charming, hateful)*

2. *(laconic, cogent, garrulous, articulate)*/word = flock/bird

3. logorrhea/words = *(drought, sprinkle, dampen, flood)*/water

4. pile/leaf = verbiage/ *(flower, coin, word, autumn)*

5. *(judge, lawyer, debater, politician)*/laconic = gossip/talkative

6. taciturn/ *(a scrooge, a storyteller, your teacher, an emcee)* = jolly/santa

7. dancing/stumbling = articulate/ *(singing, mumbling, laughing, yelling)*

8. muddy/clear = *(refreshing, amusing, convincing, confusing)*/cogent

9. died/ *(passed away, kicked the bucket, bit the dust, cashed in chips)* = plain word/euphemism

10. *(amusing, clarifying, offensive, pleasing)*/pejorative = teacher/instructor

Exercise 7 – B: Words About Words

> **Directions:** Match the words in the first column with the meanings in the second column.

Word

Clue

_____ 1. pejorative

a. a gushing *flow* of words

_____ 2. laconic

b. unneeded words

_____ 3. garrulous

c. talking a lot about little

_____ 4. logorrhea

d. talking little

_____ 5. articulate

e. okay for informal talking

_____ 6. verbiage

f. *nerd,* for example, or *hick*

_____ 7. colloquial

g. expressing ideas clearly

_____ 8. euphemism

h. *intellectually challenged,* for example

Exercise 7 – C: Write the Word

1. To avoid using words that might make people uncomfortable, I try to find a gentler term, called a/an _____.

2. Well *I'm* not worried about hurting anybody's feelings with my words. In fact, I often use words that are _____. That is, they have unpleasant or offensive connotations.

3. I talk little. I'm _____.

4. Not me. I like to use words, so when I talk or write, I use lots of them. I'm _____.

5. If you think that person back there in the preceding item, number four (4), the one before this one, which is number five (5), talks a lot, you ain't seen nothing yet. Some people talk a lot, but I talk incessantly, which is to say all the time, nonstop. You could call me

   _____.

6. Yeah, number five sure is a word-gusher, all right. There's a name for that person's condition — it's called _____.

7. Some people seem able to express themselves skillfully and easily. They are called _____. (The word is also used for speech that is clearly enunciated and pronounced.)

8. The preceding word is usually applied to *speakers* or their *language*, but this next word carries the idea that the *ideas* and *messages* are clear to the listener. A person who makes a very convincing talk may be said to have made a/an _____ argument.

9. Words are like clothes, in one way. Some are a little fancy and formal. Others words and expressions are casual — they're okay for use in easy conversation with your friends, but you wouldn't use them in speeches or business letters. These casual words and expressions are called

_____.

10. Most of us, when we write a first draft, use at least a few extra words — more than we really need to make our point. We'll improve our writing if we edit out these extra words — the ones that we call

_____.

Unit 8 – Phobias and Manias and Such

Phobias

We all have our own normal fears — some people are afraid of speaking in public (see *lalophobia*), others fear heights, spiders, snakes, and so on.

If these fears are manageable, it's a little inaccurate to call them phobias. A true phobia is much more than a reasonable fear of something dangerous — it's extreme, irrational, and persistent. It can't be explained away.

Psychologists and psychiatrists have recognized dozens of phobias. We'll look at only a sampling of some common phobias here, because if we listed too many, we might disturb anyone who suffers from *phobophobia*.

Acrophobia: This is a very common phobia. *Acro* means *end*, or *top* — as in the top of a building, mountain, or tree — places where the acrophobe surely doesn't want to be. People who suffer from *acrophobia* (ACK-ruh-FOE-bee-uh) have an uncontrollable fear of high places.

Claustrophobia: The beginning of this word sorta sounds like *close*, and that's a good clue to its meaning. People who suffer from *claustrophobia* (kloss-tro-FOE-bee-uh) can't stand to be closed in. They hate elevators, closets, even small rooms.

Agoraphobia: This one is the opposite of claustrophobia, because people with *agoraphobia* (ag-ur-uh-FOE-bee-uh or uh-GORE-uh-foe-bee-uh) have an uncontrollable fear of open spaces — like ballrooms, open fields, parking lots, or deserts.

Lalophobia: This word is not as common as others in this unit, but the phobia itself is very common. *Lalo* means *speech*, so *lalophobia* (loll-uh-FOE-bee-uh) means an abnormal fear of public speaking.

Studies have shown that many people list the fear of making a public speech as their number-one dread.

Phobophobia: There's a famous quote that goes something like this: "The only thing we have to fear is fear itself." And that's what *phobophobia* (foe-bo-FOE-bee-uh) is — unreasonable fear of being afraid. For example, people who dread public speaking may be afraid that they'll get visibly scared, and make themselves look foolish.

Ergophobia: This one (pronounced ur-go-FOE-bee-uh) was coined as a humorous usage. *Erg* means *work*, which the ergophobe (UR-go-fobe) fears. I'm not sure it's been recognized by psychologists as a real phobia, but we all know some people the word fits.

Xenophobia: The main victims of most phobias are the people who suffer from them. Unfortunately, that's not the case with *xenophobia* (zen-uh-FOE-bee-uh). *Xeno* means *stranger, foreigner,* so the word means an abnormal fear of (or hatred of) anyone or anything foreign or strange. A *xenophobe* (ZEN-o-fobe) fears people from foreign countries — and often their customs, products, music, or speech. (The term may mean fear of anyone who's different in any obvious way.)

Manias

A mania is an *abnormal* preoccupation or compulsion. (A *pyromaniac* has a compulsion to set things afire.) Psychologists use *mania* and *phobia* only in reference to persistent, irrational, conditions and attitudes. They don't apply these words to "normal" fears and fascinations.

But psychologists don't own our language, so the rest of us often use the terms freely and creatively. Someone might say a friend is an *egomaniac,* when the person is simply self-centered. Or we might call someone an *arachnephobe* simply because the person has a strong fear of spiders.

It's quite all right to do that when speaking informally. But remember that the words have a more strict definition when used in psychological contexts. With that said, let's look at a few manias and maniacs.

Egomaniac: In psychology, the term *ego* means *self*. So *egomaniacs* (ee-go-MAIN-ee-aks) are crazy about themselves. We all know egotistical people, who are merely self-centered. But egomaniacs go way beyond that. While egotists want everyone to pay attention, to listen to them, egomaniacs are obsessed with themselves. They actually think they're more important than anyone else around them. Know anybody like that? If you do, try to keep as far away as you can.

Dipsomaniac: The combining form *dipso* means *drink*, and that's pretty much what the *dipsomaniac* lives for. Dipsomania (dip-so-MAIN-ee-uh) is an abnormal craving for alcohol, an *insatiable* thirst. The line between this problem and alcoholism isn't always clear, but dipsomania may be considered more of a mental disorder.

Kleptomaniac: The first part of the word, *klepto*, means *steal*. Some people steal because they're hungry, some steal to get money for drugs or other things they want. But the *kleptomaniac* (klep-to-MAIN-ee-ack) is a compulsive thief, taking things that may not be needed, or even wanted. Some kleptomaniacs are affluent folks who could easily buy the things they steal, but they feel they *must* take things, that they have no power to resist. And they often feel invulnerable, that they can always get away with their thefts. Some do get caught, of course, and may be deeply embarrassed. Unfortunately, they often don't seek psychological help until they've been arrested.

Pyromaniac: *Pyro* means *fire*. So the *pyromaniac* is fascinated by flames, and has an irresistible urge to set things afire. (A common informal term is *firebug*.) The pyromaniac is not the same as an *arsonist* (who commits the crime of arson). The arsonist may be quite sane, if dishonest, setting fires for reasons like revenge, or to collect insurance.

Bibliomaniac: As you might guess, the *bibl* at the beginning of that word means *book*. The *bibliomaniac* (bib-lee-o-MAIN-ee-ack) is *not* just someone who happens to like books a lot, or even to love books. (That's a *bibliophile.*) The bibliomaniac has a full-blown craze for books, a compulsion to get more and more of them — not to read or pass on to others, but just to *have*. So a bibliophile may be normal, but a bibliomaniac could use a little psychological counseling.

Onomatomaniac: This word is almost always used at least half-jokingly. The onomatomaniac isn't really sick. In fact, many people don't mind the label, and even use the word in reference to themselves.

The first part of this word (*onomato*) is used much less often than most of the others we've linked up to the root *mania*. About the only fairly common word we find it in is *onomatopoeia*. (Remember, from studying poetry in English class?) Onomatopoetic words sound like what they represent — words like *swoosh, clank, clatter, hum,* or *buzz*. So *onomatomaniacs* are interested in such words, but that's only part of it. They're more than interested, they're fascinated, in love with words — all different kinds of words. They feel compelled to learn more and more words, and to learn more about them. So if you have to be some kind of maniac, this is a good kind to be.

Exercise 8 – A: Phobias and Manias

Directions: In each item below, you'll find two terms, separated by a virgule (/), that are related in some way (e.g., long/short). A third ("single") term is separated by a virgule from a series of terms in parentheses. For each item, circle the term in parentheses that has *the same relationship* to the "single" term as the paired terms have to each other.

1. acrophophobia/treetop = lalophobia/ *(writing, reading, listening, speaking)*

2. egomaniac/ *(self, others, women, men)* = workaholic/overtime

3. *(ballroom, kitchen, closet, living room)*/claustrophobic = cat/mouse

4. ghost story/child = *(friend, foreigner, brother, local person)*/xenophobe

5. kleptomaniac/ *(drinking, stealing, reading, talking)* = dipsomaniac/drinking

6. pyomaniac/fire= ergomaniac/ *(playing, talking, drinking, working)*

7. elevator/claustrophobe = *(closet, treetop, field, fire)*/agoraphobe

8. *(book, fire, self, closet)*/bibliomaniac = Hershey's kiss/chocoholic

9. robbers/cops = phobophobe/ *(work, fear, love, hate)*

10. onomatomaniac/ *(word-lover, bibliophobe, newborn baby, illiterate)* = learner/you

Exercise 8 – B: Phobias and Manias

> **Directions:** Write in each blank the letter of the word that forms the best match for that item.

Phobia   **What's Feared?**

_____ 1. acrophobia   a. speaking

_____ 2. claustrophobia   b. high places

_____ 3. agoraphobia   c. open spaces

_____ 4. lalophobia   d. closed places

_____ 5. phobophobia   e. foreigners

_____ 6. xenophobia   f. fear itself

Exercise 8 – C: Phobias and Manias

> **Directions:** Write in each blank the letter of the word that forms the best match for that item.

Who?   **Is Crazy About What?**

_____ 1. egomaniac   a. stealing

_____ 2. dipsomaniac   b. themselves

_____ 3. kleptomaniac   c. this exercise

_____ 4. pyromaniac   d. drinking

_____ 5. bibliomaniac   e. fire

_____ 6. onomatomaniac   f. books

Exercise 8 – D: Write the Word

1. I love me, I'm crazy about myself. I'm a/an _____.

2. I'm scared to death of high places. I'm a/an _____.

3. I love books, books, and more books. I'm a/an _____.

4. Please don't ask me to make a speech. I'm _____.

5. I know I shouldn't steal, but I just can't help myself. I suffer from

   _____.

6. Open spaces are what scare me. I'm a/an _____.

7. I just can't resist alcoholic drinks. I'm a/an _____.

8. Uh-oh. That person looks like a foreigner. I'm out of here, because I'm

   _____.

9. What turns me on? Flames. I'm a firebug, also known as a/an

   _____.

10. Don't fence me in, or put me in a closet. I'm _____.

11. These exercises are just too much work, and work's what I hate and
    fear. I'm _____.

12. These exercise are wonderful — all these gorgeous words. I'm a/an

    _____.

Exercise 8 – E: Write the Word

1. I hate being confined, and have a deadly fear of closets and elevators. I suffer from _____.

2. I don't mind elevators, unless they take me to a high place like a rooftop. I really fear heights, because I'm _____.

3. Do-re-*me-me-me-me*. I love me, I'm wonderful, I'm crazy about myself. I'm a/an _____.

4. I can't help taking things that don't belong to me, even if I don't need them. My problem is _____.

5. I wouldn't steal anything. Except books, of course, because I'm just crazy about books. I'm a/an _____.

6. I'm not just fond of a little drink now and then. Me, I like a big drink. I'm crazy about alcohol, so I'm called a/an _____.

7. Foreigners. I wish they'd take all their strange ways back to wherever they came from. They scare me to death. I'm _____.

8. Some people call me a firebug, because my thing is fire. I'm crazy about fires, and that's why I'm called a/an _____.

9. We've talked about a lot of words for compulsive fears, and here's one that means fear of fear itself. It's _____.

10. I love words — big words, little words, strange words, exotic words. Maybe that's why I love these exercises — because I'm a/an

_____.

Unit 9 – Words We Often Myth-Use

Even if we don't believe the old Greek and Roman myths, we've lifted a lot of useful words from them. You'll find opportunities to use these words — places where they fit your thoughts exactly. And you'll notice other people using them, in speech and writing. So knowing them will help you say what you mean, and will make you a better listener.

Here's a bonus — these words are fun. You'll be able to tell some of your friends that they're being a little *narcissistic* about their appearance. And when you complete all the jobs on your list, and your reward is *even more* jobs, you can complain that you feel like *sisyphus*.

So play with these words — have fun with them.

Tantalize: *Tantalus* (pronounced TAN-tuh-lus), was a mythical king who had offended the gods. He was condemned to stand in a pool of cool, clear water, with branches of luscious fruit just above him. But when he bent to drink, the water receded, always staying just below his mouth. And when he lifted his hand to pluck fruit, the branch bent away, keeping the fruit just out of reach. So to *tantalize* (TAN-tuh-lize) is to tease and tempt someone, but to keep the prize always out of reach.

Sisyphus: Another victim of the gods' wrath, Sisyphus (SIS-uh-fus), was also given a harsh punishment. His never-ending job was to push a huge rock up a steep hill. But when it was almost to the top, the boulder would escape his grasp and roll back down to the bottom. A difficult task that seems endless is called sisyphean (sis-uh-FEE-un).

Icarus: His father used feathers and wax to make a pair of wings for Icarus (ICK-uh-russ) to use in escaping from the island of Crete. The wings worked, but the young man flew too close to the sun, the wax melted, and he fell to his death. So people who act rashly, leaping into action without thinking first, may be called *icarian* (eye-CARE-ee-un).

Procrustes: The giant Procrustes lived in a roadside house. When a traveler passed, the giant would bring him in to spend the night in his nice bed. But Procrustes (pro-CRUSS-tees) was picky about having things fit perfectly — things like the bed and the person who slept in it. If the guest was too small, Procrustes would simply stretch him out until he fit. If any part of the guest hung over the end of the bed, the giant would simply lop it off. So a law or rule aimed at ensuring conformity at any cost is called *procrustean* (pro-CRUST-ee-un).

Narcissus: Narcissus was a handsome youth, and he knew it. He stood so long at the side of a pond, admiring his image in the water, that his feet turned into roots, and he became a flower. People who admire themselves excessively are called *narcissistic* (nar-suh-SIS-tic).

Hercules: The gods of Greek and Roman mythology sometimes came down to earth, where they might fight with humans, or make love with them. It's no wonder that Hercules (HERK-you-lees) was the strongest man on earth, because his father was the chief god Zeus (ZOOSE). Hercules did a lot of unbelievable things, including tasks that seemed impossible (the twelve labors of Hercules). So any job that seems extremely difficult may be called a *herculean* (herk-you-LEE-un) task, requiring herculean effort.

Augean: One of the labors of Hercules was to clean out the stables of King Augeas. The stables, which held 3,000 oxen, had not been cleaned in 30 years. So if you inherit a job that's been growing worse and is now a real mess, you could describe it as an *augean* (awe-GEE-un) task. (Hercules washed the stables clean by diverting a river through them.)

Scylla and Charybdis: Mythical heroes who had to sail through a narrow strait faced two great dangers: Scylla (SILL-uh) and Charybdis (kuh-RIB-dus). Scylla was a horrible six-headed monster who lived on a rock at one side of the channel. If a ship came too close, she'd grab the sailors and eat them alive.

But the ships trying to stay near the other side of the channel were endangered by Charybdis, a seething whirlpool that could suck the ships down to destruction. Sailors were at great risk to steer between them.

So if you're in a situation where there are two dangers, and avoiding one increases the risk of the other, you are between Scylla and Charybdis. We still hear this phrase, along with the modern equivalents "between a rock and a hard place," or "between the devil and the deep blue sea."

Venus: Venus, the goddess of love and beauty, was extraordinarily beautiful. So any woman who is extremely attractive may be called a *Venus* (VEE-nus), or a person with *Venusian* (vuh-NOOS-ee-un) loveliness. The second planet from the sun (we're third) is named Venus, and it's often the most beautiful sight in the evening sky.

Apollo: Apollo was the god of music, poetry, and light, among other things. He is thought of as the highest example (or apotheosis, pronounced uh-POTH-ee-O-sis) of manly beauty. A similar term is Adonis (uh-DON-us), who was described as a beautiful boy. (*Apollo* is more likely to be used for men, *Adonis* for boys or very young men.)

Aegis: The aegis was a shield carried by the Greek god Zeus. When he let someone else carry it (his daughter Athena, and sometimes Apollo), it became a symbol (and a warning) that the carrier was on Zeus's business. That's why the term *aegis* (pronounced EE-jus, sometimes spelled egis) has come to mean "sponsorship" or "auspices," as in "The poll-watchers are operating under the aegis of the election commission."

Mars: As Roman god of war, Mars gives us the name for a planet, and the word *martial* (MARSH-ull), as in martial arts and martial music. Don't confuse this word with *marital* (MARE-uh-tull), which means having to do with marriage, (as in marital bliss or marital status).

Exercise 9 – A: Words We Often Myth-Use

> **Directions:** In each item below, you'll find two terms, separated by a virgule (/), that are related in some way (e.g., long/short). A third ("single") term is separated by a virgule from a series of terms in parentheses. For each item, circle the term in parentheses that has *the same relationship* to the "single" term as the paired terms have to each other.

1. scylla/charybdis = rock/ *(first place, good place, hard place, home place)*

2. narcissus/ *(animals, self, money, music)* = altruist/others

3. young/old = *(difficult, time-consuming, demanding, easy)*/herculean

4. icarus/ *(sun, moon, stars, planets)* = daredevil/danger

5. *(filthy, clean, clear, muddy)*/augean = sterile/clean

6. mouse/trap = sisyphus/ *(hammer, sun, rock, nail)*

7. tantalize/ *(refuse, feed, agree, tempt)* = tune/melody

8. hercules/strong = procrustes/ *(agreeable, inflexible, cheery, silent)*

9. flag/banner = *(spear, horn, mace, shield)*/aegis

10. *(handsome, wealthy, peaceful, quarrelsome)*/martial = calm/frantic

Exercise 9 – B: Words We Often Myth-Use

> **Directions:** Write in each blank the letter of the word that forms the best match for that item.

Who (or What)   Is What?

_____ 1. Aegis   a. high-flyer

_____ 2. Apollo   b. a troublesome twin

_____ 3. Augean   c. self-lover

_____ 4. Charybdis   d. He's heavy into Rock and Roll

_____ 5. Herculean   e. shield of authority

_____ 6. Icarus   f. guarantees a perfect fit

_____ 7. Narcissus   g. a troublesome twin's twin

_____ 8. Procrustes   h. supernatural beauty

_____ 9. Scylla   i. handsome man

_____10. Sisyphus   j. super-filthy

_____11. Venus   k. big, big job

Exercise 9 – C: Write the Word

1. My room's so messy, it looks like the _____ stables.

2. Flexible rules can be good, but our rule-makers, like _____, want everything to be the same for everyone.

3. Wow, that woman/man's really beautiful/handsome. She/he looks like _____/_____.

4. Of course, *I'm* much better looking. Like _____, I love to admire myself.

5. I guess my appearance just _____s all those people I flirt with, but don't let get too close.

6. I have a press pass, so you could say I'm traveling under the _____ of the media.

7. When you push your luck by doing something dangerous, you're being like _____.

8. When you have two choices and don't like either one, you're between _____.

9. Learning words is fun, but sometimes I have so much homework I feel I'm being asked to perform the labors of _____.

10. I learn all these words, and then the teacher gives me another batch. Sometimes I feel like _____, forever rolling his rock.

Unit 10 – Animal Words

Have you ever been searching for just the right word to describe someone — the person's shape, or appearance, or movements — and realized that the person reminds you of some kind of animal? Big, unblinking eyes like a fish, or the body shape of a duck, or the graceful movements of a cat? We've all seen cats move, and we instantly get a clear mental image of the animal's smooth, sinuous movements. The following words, from animal names or features, can be used in complimentary ways, neutral ways, or pejorative ways. We could talk about the quickness of a fox (complimentary), the hair-color of a fox (neutral), or the deceitful trickiness of a fox (pejorative).

These words, like other useful tools, can be dangerous, so use them with care. We don't want to offend anyone unintentionally.

Bovine: You know some exciting, active, interesting people — folks who always seem to be doing something. And then at the other extreme are people who just stand around like cattle chewing their cuds. They're dull, uninterested in much of anything, and uninteresting. Such people are *bovine* (BO-vine), from the Latin word for ox or cow.

Ursine: *Ursine* (UR-sine) people are big, often friendly, maybe not too neat in appearance or dress. They have a sort of bear-like quality about them. (The root *Ursa* means *bear*, and there are two constellations of stars called Ursa major — the big bear — and Ursa minor — the little bear.)

Vulpine: This word (pronounced VUL-pine) means *foxlike*. It can be used to describe someone's appearance, or the cunning and somewhat tricky way the fox's mind works.

Equine: This word, pronounced EE-qwine, refers to horses and their relatives (donkeys, mules, zebras). *Equestrian* (ee-KWESS-tree-un) can mean a person who rides horses, and can also mean "having to do with horses," like equestrian arts.

Leonine: The root *Leo* means *lion*. If we hear that someone has a *leonine* (LEE-o-nine) appearance, we might think of an expansive manelike head of hair, or an upright posture and carriage that suggests pride.

Piscine: The word *piscine* (PIE-seen) applies to a person who reminds us of a fish. We probably don't use this word as often as some of the others (like *leonine*), but there are times when it's exactly the word to describe an unblinking, wide-eyed gaze. (Pisces is the zodiac sign of the fish.)

Feline: This one, of course, means having something to do with *cats*. It can be an adjective (she moved with *feline* grace) or a noun (lions and tigers are felines). It's pronounced FEE-line.

Canine: The word *canine* means *dog*, or doglike. It has a wide variety of uses — neutral, favorable, and unfavorable. We can speak of canine cunning, canine loyalty, or canine shape. (Those pointy teeth just beside our front teeth are called canines, because they resemble a dog's teeth.)

Porcine: This word (pronounced POR-sine or POR-s'n) looks a little like *pork*, and means *piglike*, or having something to do with pigs. "I've got to go on a diet — I'm beginning to look absolutely *porcine*."

Anthropoid: Well, fair's fair. So if we're looking at all these words about animals, we should probably include one that works the other way around. *Anthropoid* (ANTHRUH-poid) means like or resembling a *human*. We often use this one to describe animals (and sometimes robots or computers). We could speak of an anthropoid ape (one shaped like a human), or we might say that a fox seemed to have anthropoid intelligence. The word comes from *anthropos*, which is also found in *anthropology* (the study of the distribution and social customs of humans).

Exercise 10 – A: Animal Words

Directions: In each item below, you'll find two terms, separated by a virgule (/), that are related in some way (e.g., long/short). A third ("single") term is separated by a virgule from a series of terms in parentheses. For each item, circle the term in parentheses that has *the same relationship* to the "single" term as the paired terms have to each other.

1. gluttonous/pig = leonine/ *(fish, lion, whale, snake)*

2. horse-racing/ *(equine, porcine, avian, bovine)* = dog-racing/canine

3. hunter/prey = *(piscine, equine, bovine, feline)*/mouse

4. porcine/ *(chubby, tall, lanky, strong)* = svelte/slim

5. *(milk, honey, sugar, biscuit)*/bovine = eggs/fowl

6. canine/loyal = vulpine/ *(dumb, crafty, greedy, brave)*

7. *(hound, trout, thoroughbred, siamese)*/piscine = sophomore/student

8. canine/ *(fish, birds, ants, cats)* = feline/mice

9. toy horse/equine = robot/ *(piscine, vulpine, anthropoid, bovine)*

10. piggish/greedy = leonine/ *(brave, gentle, wily, lazy)*

Exercise 10 – B: Animals, Mostly

> **Directions:** Write in each blank the letter of the word that forms the best match for that item.

Word

Clue

_____ 1. anthropoid

a. sly and crafty

_____ 2. bovine

b. horsing around

_____ 3. canine

c. this little piggy

_____ 4. equine

d. bear with me on this one

_____ 5. feline

e. sounds fishy to me

_____ 6. leonine

f. king of the jungle

_____ 7. piscine

g. man's best friend

_____ 8. porcine

h. pretty catty

_____ 9. ursine

i. ever heard of cattle?

_____ 10. vulpine

j. dog's best friend

Exercise 10 – C: Write the Word

1. The actor's huge mane of hair gave him a _____
   look.

2. The other actor, who played dumb, just stood there looking cowlike,
   with a _____ expression on his face.

3. The actress moved with the _____ grace of a
   leopard.

4. The police unit that uses dogs is named after these animals:
   _____.

5. The wrestler looked somewhat bearlike, with ambling,
   _____ movements.

6. One character in *Lord of the Flies* was called "Piggy" because of his
   _____ appearance.

7. The gambler's crafty expression and pointed ears made his face look
   _____.

8. The statue's rounded eyes and pouting, fishlike mouth gave her face
   a/an _____ expression.

9. Horses, donkeys, and zebras are among the _____
   animals.

10. _____ animals resemble humans.

Unit 11 – A Few Foreign Words and Phrases

Americans are notorious logoklepts — we'll steal any interesting word that's left lying around loose. We've already looked at some of the words stolen from Greek and Latin. Now let's look at some other verbal loot from foreign languages, mostly French. As usual, you'll find suggested pronunciations for each word or phrase. But when words are taken from another language, it's almost impossible for anyone who didn't grow up speaking the language to pronounce the word exactly the way a native speaker would. That's okay. People of other languages have a lot of trouble with English, so don't worry about it. And don't be xenophobic about these foreign terms. Just do the best you can with the pronunciation, and have fun with the phrases.

Carpé diem: This Latin phrase literally means "seize the day," but a good working translation would be something like "take advantage of whatever opportunity you see at hand," or "strike while the iron is hot." It's pronounced something like car-pay-DEE-um. So with this as your motto, you'll want to learn all the words you can.

C'est la vie, c'est la guerre: You might use the phrase *c'est la vie* with upturned palms and a shrug, after something happened that you had no control over — if the rain spoiled your picnic, or your teacher had to postpone the test you were looking forward to, for example. It's pronounced say-la-VEE, and may be translated "such is life."

The phrase *c'est la guerre* (say-la-GEAR) means "such is war." You'd be more likely to use it in regard to some kind of competition, like an athletic contest. If you trounce your opponent (or vice versa), you could just say "Well, *c'est la guerre.*"

Faux pas: Oops. You made a mistake? Another term for a clumsy goof — especially a social blunder, is *faux pas*, which is French for "false step." It's pronounced FOE-PAH.

Carte blanche: Some supervisors and teachers are very strict, demanding that everything be done just their way. Then on the other hand, there are people like *your* teacher, who give you a lot of freedom in how you do the job — as long as you get it done. If you want freedom and personal responsibility in your work, you'd enjoy *carte blanche* (cart BLANH-sh). The words literally mean "blank card," so if someone gives you carte blanche, it means you can write your own ticket, that you have almost complete freedom to do as you like.

Chacun à son goût: If people make fun of you or someone else who doesn't do things the way they would, you could answer *chacun à son goût* (shack-un-ah-son-GOO). The phrase means "each to his own taste," and an American version might be "different strokes for different folks."

Coup de grâce, coup d'état: A *coup de grâce* (coo-duh-GRAHS) is the final, masterful stroke which puts an end to something (or someone). The phrase literally means "stroke of mercy," and in the old days, it was used to mean the death blow delivered to a suffering victim. But now it's most often used in less serious ways. If a tennis player serves a series of aces to end a match that had worn her opponent down, you could say she had delivered the *coup de grâce* to the loser.

The word *coup* means "stroke," so *coup d'état* could be translated "stroke of the state." It's most often used to mean the sudden, decisive action taken to overthrow a ruler or government.

Déjà Vu: Have you ever been somewhere for the first time, or done something you've never done before, yet had the distinct (often eerie) feeling that you'd had the experience before? Psychologists call that a feeling of *déjà vu* (DAY-ZHA-VOO), which literally means "already seen."

Esprit de corps: This phrase literally means "spirit of the body, or group." A decent translation into our language would be "team spirit." It's the pride that members of a group (team, nation, etc.) have in themselves and other members. And a decent pronunciation is uh-spree-duh-COR.

Verboten: This word is applied to something *forbidden*, something that is taboo or against a law or regulation. It's *verboten* (fur-BOAT'n) to skinny-dip in the city fountain, or to hunt or fish out of season.

Joie de vivre: Okay, let's end our list on a positive note. The foreign phrase *joie de vivre* (zhwah-de-VEEV) may be a little hard to say, but it's useful and fun. And there's no common phrase in our language that quite expresses the thought. It means the "joy of living," the gladness of simply being alive. Most of us admire this quality in others, and desire it for ourselves. We might say "I like being around Rachel, because she has so much *joie de vivre* that she always brightens up my day."

Exercise 11 – A: Foreign Words and Phrases

> **Directions:** In each item below, you'll find two terms, separated by a virgule (/), that are related in some way (e.g., long/short). A third ("single") term is separated by a virgule from a series of terms in parentheses. For each item, circle the term in parentheses that has *the same relationship* to the "single" term as the paired terms have to each other.

1. look before you leap/caution = carpé diem/ *(opportunity, money, mistake, taboo)*

2. c'est la vie/ *(war, taste, self, life)* = c'est la guerre/war

3. *(true, false, old, young)*/faux pas = real/actual

4. released/confined = carte blanche/ *(liberated, unconfined, controlled, free)*

5. chacun à son goût/personal choice = *(different, varying, same, random)*/ uniform

6. joie de vivre/ *(sorrow, pleasure, anger, regret)* = prevaricating/lying

7. déjà vu/ *(report, later, already, vision)* = echo/hearing

8. spirit/enthusiasm = *(patriotism, hatred, laziness, sloppiness)*/esprit de corps

9. compliment/kind = faux pas/ *(skilled, clumsy, easy, hard)*

10. verboten/ *(nice, clumsy, permitted, forbidden)* = illegal/allowed

Exercise 11 – B: Foreign Words and Phrases

> **Directions:** Write in each blank the letter of the word that forms the best match for that item.

Phrase	Clue
_____ 1. c'est la vie	a. Our word-learning team is the greatest
_____ 2. c'est la guerre	b. Been there, done that
_____ 3. carpé diem	c. The final stroke
_____ 4. carte blanche	d. Oops, I goofed.
_____ 5. chacun à son goût	e. Well, that's life.
_____ 6. coup de grâce	f. Take advantage of an opportunity
_____ 7. coup d'etat	g. Taking control of the government.
_____ 8. déjà vu	h. Old soldiers might say "Well, war's like that."
_____ 9. esprit de corps	i. We'll have a free hand to do what we like.
_____ 10. faux pas	j. Isn't life just grand?
_____ 11. joie de vivre	k. Different strokes for different folks

Exercise 11 – C: Write the Word

1. Another exercise? I have a feeling of _____, as if I've been here before.

2. Isn't life great? If you think so, you have a lot of _____.

3. If you don't think so, you're entitled to your own opinion. As they say, "different strokes for different folks," or _____ .

4. If things don't go as planned, I say _____, or "that's life."

5. If my team plays a tough game and loses, we say _____, or "that's war."

6. Do I have _____ to write in any phrase I want?

7. No. If I write in the wrong one, the teacher may say I made a/an

   _____.

8. My motto is _____, so I'll seize the opportunity to do well on this exercise.

9. A stroke that finishes someone (e.g., a suffering victim) is called a/an

   _____.

10. A surprise move to take over a government is called a/an

    _____.

11. My team is great, I know we'll do well on this exercise. We have a lot of _____.

Unit 12 – Going on From Here

In working through this book, you've probably learned more words than most adults do in years. That's a lot of progress in a short time, and you don't want to backslide now that you're on your own again. We suggest you choose (and use) some of the following methods to keep building your vocabulary. Pick the ones you'll enjoy (otherwise you're less likely to practice them).

Use the Dictionary

This sounds almost too simple to mention, doesn't it? But it's important, it's often neglected, and it takes a little discipline and continuing practice.

So make sure you have a good dictionary, and keep it handy (even onomatomaniacs won't walk across the room every time they come across a new word — they'll say, "I'll look it up later," but they'll forget it). Get in the habit of reaching for it every time you find a word you're not sure about. Using the dictionary is habit forming — it gets easier with practice.

Tap Into Your Computer

If you have access to a computer, or to someone who does and is also interested in words, you can keep a running list of new words. You're creating your own personal dictionary.

Your electronic lexicographer will sort the words alphabetically, and you can add your own mnemonic devices (memory aids), pronunciation tips, and anything else you want.

Sample Some Other Books

There are other good books available, so browse through a few libraries and bookstores. Pick up the vocabulary books, flip through a few pages, read a few exercises. Chances are you'll find one or two that will work for you. (And while you're looking, you just might steal a word or two — there's nothing wrong with being a logoklept.)

The person at the reference desk of your local library can also recommend some good books, or point out the best shelves for you to browse through.

Become a Bookie

Nobody else's words are exactly the ones you want to learn. So you may want to buy a small spiral notebook to start your own list.

Writing down new words will take some discipline, but it really pays off, and can become fun as you look at the growing list of words you're learning. Use the lined pages at the back of this book ("Adding To Your Idiolect") as a start. Remember, it's *your idiolect*, and you're the best judge of which words you want to add to it.

Become a Word-Gamester

You'll probably enjoy playing some word games like scrabble, crosswords, acrostics, jumbles, hangman, and several others. For some reason, most wordhounds seem to like some of these and dislike others. So try them all — you'll probably learn to like (or like better) at least one or two.

Note: We don't think word-gaming is the best way to make big, quick gains in your vocabulary. There's a lot of repetition, and you'll learn words you'll rarely use anywhere else. (How often do you need the name of a three-toed sloth?) But they do help keep up interest in words, and that helps you keep building your word power.

Take A Course

Look around for a course in vocabulary development, or something similar. You'll learn enough to make it worthwhile, and it will give your interest level a boost.

Keep Reading — Keep Listening

The words you're most likely to need — and therefore the words of most value to you — will come from your everyday reading and listening. Read good newspapers and good magazines. Read about your hobbies and your work. Listen to good radio and TV programs, and listen to your friends and co-workers. Stay alert for new and interesting words. If you do, you'll always be increasing your vocabulary — and having fun.

Adding To Your Idiolect

Term	Meaning	Example, Notes
Logorrhea	Extreme wordiness	He has a bad case of logorrhea.

Term	Meaning	Example, Notes
nugatory	trivial, unimportant	Too many people spend their time on nugatory activities.

Term	Meaning	Example, Notes

Answer Key

People and Their Personalities
1-A: 1. introvert, 2. self-centeredness, 3. luxury-lover, 4. woman-lover, 5. shy guy, 6. hermit, 7. woman-hater, 8. most, 9. hermit, 10. luddite
1-B: 1. d, 2. f, 3. h, 4. j, 5. a, 6. g, 7. b, 8. i, 9. c, 10. e
1-C: 1. misogynist, 2. misogamist, 3. misanthrope, 4. altruist, 5. luddite, 6. introvert, 7. extrovert, 8. voluptuary, 9. ascetic, 10. recluse

It's About Time
2-A: 1. sidereal, 2. thousand, 3. owls, 4. delay, 5. sequel, 6. twilight, 7. contemporary, 8. dinosaur, 9. century, 10. at the same time
2-B: 1. i, 2. f, 3. b, 4. j, 5. h, 6. e, 7. c, 8. d, 9. g, 10. a
2-C: 1. procrastinator, 2. anachronistic, 3. nocturnal, 4. sequel, 5. fin de siecle, 6. diurnal, 7. anachronism, 8. synchronous, 9. precedent, 10. crepuscular

About Money
3-A: 1. frugal, 2. destitute, 3. philanthropist, 4. opulence, 5. affluence, 6. fiscal, 7. lucre, 8. penurious, 9. profligate, 10. avarice
3-B: 1. i, 2. f, 3. b, 4. h, 5. d, 6. c, 7. e, 8. g, 9. j, 10. a
3-C: 1. frugal, 2. parsimonious (penurious)*, 3. opulent, 4. destitute (penurious)*, 5. avaricious, 6. profligate, 7. philanthropist, 8. parsimonious (penurious)*, 9. fiscal, 10. affluent. *NOTE: "Penurious" is sometimes used in this sense, but actually means "poor."

Health Practitioners
4-A: 1. eyes, 2. gynecologist, 3. dermatologist, 4. optician, 5. vision, 6. children, 7. neurologist, 8. orthodontist, 9. heart, 10. pregnancy
4-B: 1. h, 2. e, 3. k, 4. o (or k), 5. a, 6. f, 7. b, 8. m, 9. j, 10. c, 11. d, 12. n, 13. g, 14. i, 15. l
4-C: 1. diagnosis, 2. women, 3. pregnancy, childbirth, 4. children, 5. skin, 6. eyes, 7. heart, 8. nerves, 9. mental, emotional problems, 10. feet, 11. straightens teeth, 12. measures vision, 13. grinds lenses, 14. eyes, 15. children's teeth
4-D: 1. gynecologist, 2. dermatologist, 3. optometrist, 4. optician, 5. ophthamologist/oculist, 6. cardiologist, 7. obstetrician, 8. pedodontist, 9. orthodontist, 10. psychiatrist

Who's in Charge Here?
5-A: 1. g, 2. m, 3. a, 4. j, 5. b, 6. e, 7. h, 8. i, 9. n, 10. c, 11. k, 12. l, 13. f, 14. d
5-B: 1. the people, 2. representatives, 3. church, 4. king, 5. worst, 6. rich, 7. university, 8. nobody, 9. kinfolk, 10. ochlocracy
5-C: 1. democracy, 2. republic, 3. plutocracy, 4. meritocracy, 5. theocracy, 6. militocracy, 7. anarchy, 8. ochlocracy, 9. nepotism, 10. kakistocracy

Sciences and Pseudosciences
6-A: 1. people, 2. horoscope, 3. bumps, 4. cave, 5. bones, 6. handwriting, 7. lava, 8. living things, 9. giraffe, 10. insects
6-B: 1. phrenologist, 2. astronomy, 3. geologist, 4. biologist, 5. zoologist, 6. botanist, 7. entomologist, 8. astrologer, 9. graphologist, 10. anthropologist

6-C: 1. people, 2. heavenly bodies (stars, planets, etc.), 3. earth, 4. volcanos, 5. head bumps (shapes, etc.), 6. living things, 7. heavenly bodies' influence on lives, 8. handwriting, 9. animals, 10. plants, 11. insects

Words About Words
7-A: 1. quiet, 2. garrulous, 3. flood, 4. word, 5. judge, 6. a scrooge, 7. mumbling, 8. confusing, 9. passed away, 10. offensive
7-B: 1. f, 2. d, 3. c, 4. a, 5. g, 6. b, 7. e, 8. h
7-C: 1. euphemism, 2. pejorative, 3. laconic, 4. verbose, 5. garrulous, 6. logorrhea, 7. articulate, 8. cogent, 9. colloquial, 10. verbiage

Phobias and Manias and Such
8-A: 1. speaking, 2. self, 3. closet, 4. foreigner, 5. stealing, 6. working, 7. field, 8. book, 9. fear, 10. word-lover
8-B: 1. b, 2. d, 3. c, 4. a, 5. f, 6. e
8-C: 1. b, 2. d, 3. a, 4. e, 5. f, 6. c
8-D: 1. egomaniac, 2. acrophobe, 3. bibliomaniac, 4. lalophobic, 5. kleptomania, 6. agoraphobe, 7. dipsomaniac, 8. xenophobic, 9. pyromaniac, 10. claustrophobic, 11. ergophobic, 12. onomatomaniac
8-E: 1. claustrophobia, 2. acrophobic, 3. egomaniac, 4. kleptomania, 5. biblioklept, bibliomaniac, 6. dipsomaniac, 7. xenophobic, 8. pyromaniac, 9. phobophobia, 10. onomatomaniac

Words We Often Myth-Use
9-A: 1. hard place, 2. self, 3. easy, 4. sun, 5. filthy, 6. rock, 7. tempt, 8. inflexible, 9. shield, 10. peaceful
9-B: 1. e, 2. i, 3. j, 4. b/g, 5. k, 6. a, 7. c, 8. f, 9. g/b, 10. d, 11.h. NOTE: Scylla and Charybdis, are interchangeable.
9-C: 1. Augean, 2. Procrustes, 3. Venus/Apollo, 4. Narcissus, 5. tantalize, 6. aegis, 7. Icarus, 8. Scylla and Charybdis, 9. Hercules, 10. Sisyphus

Animal Words
10-A: 1. lion, 2. equine, 3. feline, 4. chubby, 5. milk, 6. crafty, 7. trout, 8. cats, 9. anthropoid, 10. brave
10-B: 1. j, 2. i, 3. g, 4. b, 5. h, 6. f, 7. e, 8. c, 9. d, 10. a
10-C: 1. leonine, 2. bovine, 3. feline, 4. canine/K-9, 5. ursine, 6. porcine, 7. vulpine, 8. piscine, 9. equine, 10, anthropoid

A Few Foreign Words and Phrases
11-A: 1. opportunity, 2. life, 3. false, 4. controlled, 5. same, 6. pleasure, 7. vision, 8. patriotism, 9. clumsy, 10. permitted. Note: "prevaricating" (in item 6) means "telling an untruth, lying, fibbing."
11-B: 1. e, 2. h, 3. f, 4. i, 5. k, 6. c, 7. g, 8. b, 9. a, 10. d, 11. j
11-C: 1. déjà vu, 2. joie de vivre, 3. chacun à son goût, 4. c'est la vie, 5. c'est la guerre, 6. carte blanche, 7. faux pas, 8. carpé diem, 9. coup de grâce, 10. coup d'ètat, 11. esprit de corps

Printed in the United States
46143LVS00003B/4